Praise for Reversing Entropy

In her newest collection, *Reversing Entropy*, Luci Shaw sings a "benediction/ of beauty" where "[g]race comes in every/gather of green" and "contraries . . . join all the making/and remaking/within the fluid universe." Her rituals of observation and creation—be it hiking, knitting, photography, or writing— interweave the natural and spiritual. The darkened woods we stumble through lead to the lake, where "the moon's doubled/image drowns us in soft light." In these wise and wonderous poems, the poet ponders how to hold onto memory and how to let it go. Beginning with her affirmation "the body, that ancient house for the soul . . . spins toward ultimate healing," she also meditates on faith, relationships, and aging, allowing space for grief and questions. Most essentially—in a life that chooses energy over entropy—Luci Shaw celebrates creatures, creatives, and the Creator, vowing "to live like the cedar tree in the psalm /. . . to never / let the years hinder my going and my growing." May it be so. *Reversing Entropy* astutely mentors us for a thriving and enduring life.
—*Marjorie Maddox,* author of *Begin with a Question*

"Every lost word will recall its meaning," Luci Shaw begins in this, her latest volume, all "restored to its place in a poem." How often she has reminded us that what "seems mundane and trivial may show itself to be a holy, precious part of a pattern," I think of the poems of Gerard Manley Hopkins when I enter her poems. How often she has captured the light shining in and through the things of our world, her scintillant music transforming what is there before us, there in the stars and at our feet in the sand and pebbles and motes around us. With her photographer's trained eye she humbly reveals again and again the incredible abundance of God's plentitude. And for that gift, so gracefully and abundantly bestowed, I thank and praise her.
—*Paul Mariani,* author of *The Mystery of It All: The Vocation of Poetry in the Twilight of Modernity*

Reversing Entropy incarnates what Luci Shaw's long life gives record to: that all things are transformed, from leaf to dirt, from lost words to new poem; from shadow to light. For her the order of the universe is the re-ordering of disorder. As in the past, so these newest poems are almost preternaturally attuned to the changes and always changing natural world—the slow growth of lichens; the quick migrating flights of starlings. Luci Shaw's poems and life have been lived in faithfulness to the gift of the world around us, a gift intimately connected to the gift of words, to the making and remaking that goes on and on. She is a woman utterly open to the annunciations of starlight, to the "music" of fragrant lilies of the valley, to the exuberance of spring green leaf-light. She has lived her life

according to one abiding principle: let wherever you find yourself be a place of opportunity rather than disappointment. These new poems exemplify what it means to be present, to live in a state of readiness for whatever comes next.
—**Robert Cording,** author of *In the Unwalled City*

Those who love Luci Shaw's earlier poems will find in these a familiar, welcoming openness to the light that shines from every leaf and the voice that speaks in wind. In these her attentiveness to the created order extends to other dimensions of awareness—of her own longings and losses, of the scope of small pleasures, of how acceptance gentles the challenges of aging and of the learning that happens in moments of letting go. Images and words linger long after putting the book down and widen like ripples on waters disturbed by a soft breeze.
—**Marilyn McEntyre,** author of *Caring for Words in a Culture of Lies, When Poets Pray,* and *Speaking Peace in a Climate of Conflict*

In *Reversing Entropy*, Luci Shaw takes a stand with eternity against the passing of mortal time. In poems that by turn lament and accept the evening of her many days, she is able to feel "the dark at its deepest" while remaining her "flush, fresh, living" self. She makes me hope that all of us, as we age and slow, will still be "like kids waiting / to go outside for recess." There, on that far playground, "shadow will be consumed by the wide mouth of light."
—**Paul J. Willis,** author of *Somewhere to Follow*

Luci Shaw in *Reversing Entropy,* her new book of luminous poems, confronts chaos and plague, indeed, old age and death, and rolls them back on themselves, discovering when she does that "beauty will not be / always dimmed, no matter how long it waits." Throughout the lyrical collection, Shaw "[p]airs the antonyms / energy and entropy," as she tries to recapture each "lost word," recognizes she's "never been this old before," and grieves the loss of her only sibling whose "jagged narrative of a life" is "a cold meal . . . flavored with bitter herbs." In so doing, she explores the lichen's underworld, mountain trails, whales and weeds, even a Sequoia "thick as God's arm," so that with her, we can see how "[g]reen / gushes from every notch and knot" and "sunlight winks its enchantment." In reflecting upon all that she has weathered, Shaw's signature voice invites us to feel the "torn tissues / ragged blemishes" of "[f]ailures" and "regrets," yet pin our hope on the "gleaming fabric of / metaphors" and the "tenacious / truths . . . that will not fade like breath on a / mirror." How can we possibly say no?
—**Julie L. Moore**, author of *Full Worm Moon*

Luci Shaw is the patron saint of wonder. She writes of needing to be there, in creation, like a journalist taking field notes. And we need her to be there, too, "holding all the world-loveliness . . . by pinning it in print on paper." Of all the loveliness she's captured, over many decades, this might be her best collection yet.
—*Sarah Arthur,* author of *A Light So Lovely: The Spiritual Legacy of Madeleine L'Engle*

Reversing Entropy

Poems

Luci Shaw

IRON
PEN

PARACLETE PRESS
BREWSTER, MASSACHUSETTS

2024 First Printing

Reversing Entropy: Poems

Copyright © 2024 by Luci Shaw

ISBN 978-1-64060-870-2

The Iron Pen name and logo are trademarks of Paraclete Press.

Library of Congress Cataloging-in-Publication Data
Names: Shaw, Luci, author.
Title: Reversing entropy : poems / Luci Shaw.
Description: Brewster, Massachusetts : Iron Pen/Paraclete Press, [2024] |
Summary: "Poems that are created in the face of entropy, because the
Earth is so very beautiful and to be celebrated"— Provided by
publisher.
Identifiers: LCCN 2023024898 (print) | LCCN 2023024899 (ebook) | ISBN
9781640608702 (trade paperback) | ISBN 9781640608719 (epub) | ISBN
9781640608726 (pdf)
Subjects: LCGFT: Poetry.
Classification: LCC PS3569.H384 R48 2024 (print) | LCC PS3569.H384
(ebook) | DDC 892.8--dc23/eng/20230526
LC record available at https://lccn.loc.gov/2023024898
LC ebook record available at https://lccn.loc.gov/2023024899

10 9 8 7 6 5 4 3 2 1

Published by Paraclete Press
Brewster, Massachusetts
www.paracletepress.com

Printed in the United States of America

My profound gratitude goes to
Karen Cooper,
who understands my undisciplined methods
of creation and composition,
cuts to the heart of a metaphor,
or helps me to clean up a disorderly line of verse.

PROLOGUE
REVERSING ENTROPY
(Definition and Description)

Entropy: A measure of the molecular disorder, or randomness, of a system, its lack of order or predictability, resulting in a gradual decline into disorder.

Our universe, and the systems within it, constantly shift from their created states of order towards disorder, or chaos. The second law of thermodynamics asserts that entropy, or disorder, always increases with time. Creative human activities such as art, architecture, music, story, or film are human efforts to halt and reverse this loss of meaning. Thus, smaller systems, like individual poems, become highly ordered as they receive energy from outside themselves, from the poet. They *reverse entropy* because they are moving from a state of disorder (all the random ideas, words, and phrases available to the writer) into an orderly form designed by the writer to create meaningful images and concepts in the reader's mind (which is where the word "imag-ination" comes from.) This transfer of images, concepts, and ideas into the mind of a reader is the task of poetry and the calling of the poet. Just as a composer of music gathers rhythms, notes, melodies, or harmony, organizing them into fugues or sonatas or concertos, so poets work and write to discover ways of arranging their responses to the world in words that introduce meaning and beauty in the mind of the reader.

Which is what I've been trying to do for most of my life.

FOREWORD

by Paula Huston

Now 95, Luci Shaw has been and still is a powerful exemplar for countless younger people. Her wisdom has been hard-earned through unflinching attention to life's challenges and insights, and in this latest collection, *Reversing Entropy,* she takes one of humanity's unchanging questions, how and why do we go on creating art, knowing that dissolution and mortality are inevitable.

One compelling reason is that the earth, and all its creatures, is so incontrovertibly beautiful. A passionate lover of nature—herons, tulips, beach pebbles—she celebrates but never romanticizes the geological and biological miracles that surround her.

Like Mary Oliver she is a keen observer and recorder of nature, seeking the perfect handfuls of words to convey what she sees. In one poem, for example, she speaks of "a minor startle of white lilies rising from the valley of their green leaves." In another, she captures the effect of wind on water: "Under a brief breeze, the little lake shivers." Without anthropomorphizing she acknowledges our powerful human connection with water, stone, and sky: "How oceans love the generous energies of storms that surge them into frothy delirium."

Another reason we create in the face of entropy, she believes, is because we can preserve with words what is otherwise ephemeral. Like Keats, she understands that there's a poignant undertone to our delight in the loveliness of dew-covered grasses. In fact, our response is actually heightened by the fact that this beauty is fleeting. As she points out in one poem, "love and living move away, diminish. A breaking wave sweeps and cleanses the beach." Our mortality urges us to take delight in whatever of beauty and meaning we can find, wherever we can find it. Sometimes what is achingly beautiful manifests and disappears within seconds: "The sky in the east breaks open, the fervent color of a pomegranate." At other times we stand stunned in the face of beauty's dissolution: "the chill of loss extends to the tips of the fingers. Sorrow's breathing is a gulp of dark air with a hint of smoke."

According to Luci, we continue to create in the face of entropy because, in spite of the reality of death, the earth is so very beautiful, and because this gift of delight in loveliness is ephemeral, to be celebrated while we have it.

Writing about it can become a way to preserve and cherish that fragile, mutable loveliness. *How* we do this requires what Simone Weil calls the spiritual discipline of "attention"—a reverent, ego-less gaze upon that which simply *is*. Luci uses Weil's term in one of her poems, "Days like this, when the light is right, its glints dilate the pupil of my attention, I drink in the brightness like lemonade." In other poems she attends to the smallest details: ". . . last night's rain glitters in the drainage ditch roadside, a river of mirrors—a map of light." And tulips ". . . thrust up their fierce, purple beaks."

What happens when we attend to experience this way? Like the author of the fourteenth-century mystical treatise *The Cloud of Unknowing*, Luci intuits that what we experience in nature is meant to point us beyond—that there is a "world behind the world" to which we have brief access. Her poetry is thus often sacramental; what we see and touch are outward and visible signs of deeper realities. Sometimes she simply says this out loud: "a mist drifts like a spirit over the lake at evening." Elsewhere she is more indirect: "with what calm and gentle grace last night's fresh poem of snow was laid across the land." On still other occasions, she boldly knocks at the door between the two worlds, asking to be let in. "Below, we listen deep, praying to be some drop in some wave, urged on by the strong winds of the Weather-Maker."

What a felicitous gift *Reversing Entropy* turns out to be. May it bless others as it has already blessed me.

Paula Huston
Big Sur, September 20, 2022

CONTENTS

Prologue: Reversing Entropy / 8

Foreword by Paula Huston / 9

I
MY BRIGHT, PARTICULAR STAR

My Bright, Particular Star / 18

Bird Words / 20

Whisper / 21

Lilies of the Valley / 22

Moving the Dogwood / 23

Scarlet / 24

Just Add Water / 25

Breeze / 27

The Dance of the Lichens / 28

Exuberance, Mt. Baker National Forest / 30

Driving Through the Season / 31

Crossing the Cascades / 33

Look Up / 35

Lake Light / 36

The Apricot Tree / 37

Waiting for the Ferry 1 / 39

Waiting for the Ferry 2 / 40

New Leaf Restaurant / 41

Creek-side / 43

Whale / 44

In the Mist / 45

Gingko Leaves / 46

One Leaf, November / 47

The Star in the Kitchen Window / 48

How Lucky / 49

Saturday Afternoon, Waiting for the Mail / 50

Knitting in the Wild / 52

In a Field / 53

Above Taos Gorge / 54

Universe / 56

II
WEATHERING

Cicada Night / 58

Fresh / 59

Waiting for Words / 60

How It Happens / 61

Stones / 62

Sudden / 63

Laundry List / 64

Woman in Blue / 65

New Poem / 66

So Much Depends / 67

Sequoia / 69

Weathering / 70

December / 71

III
THE FALL TO EARTH

Mary and the Angel / 74

The Hope of Glory / 76

Snow / 77

Mary's Sword / 78

A Child's Questions / 80

Scant / 81

Jesus Tells His Story / 83

IV
ENERGY & ENTROPY

Energy & Entropy / 86

To Do / 87

Older / 88

Track / 89

Out Walking / 90

Island, Spring 2022 / 91

Surprise / 93

Grace / 94

Level / 95

Enlightened / 96

V

LOVE IN THE TIME OF PLAGUE

Brass Tray / 98

Flight / 99

What to Admire / 100

Primeval / 101

Responses / 103

Heartwood / 104

Love in the Time of Plague / 105

Up Close / 106

Intermission / 107

VI

FINAL BREATH

Remembering Rosalind / 110

In memory of my brother,

John Henry Northcote Deck. 1932–2022

1 Leaving / 112

2 Final Breath / 113

3 The Sift of Grief / 115

4 On the Death of my Brother / 116

5 Aftermath / 117

6 The Boats, the Beach / 118

7 After the Storm / 119

Clues for Perception / 120

The Quickening: To Be Sung in Procession to Heaven's Gate / 122

Acknowledgments / 126

I

~

MY BRIGHT, PARTICULAR STAR

MY BRIGHT, PARTICULAR STAR

At night, the clear skylight
in my bedroom ceiling
invites me to look up, to see
beyond ceiling, beyond cloud,
beyond sky, into deep space.

It is a clear night
when the first message,
a pinprick of light from beyond
arrives, compels my observation,
calls me to look up again,
to keep looking up, to join in
a kind of dialog with one
incandescent star.

Her signals arrive from far,
to near, to far again,
searching me out.

My "bright, particular star,"
a phrase from Shakespeare,
is the title I've given this sweet
stab to the soul that speaks
from outer space
into my room, my life.

I sleep. Wake. Look again.
The little star has wandered.
She winks, now, from the frame's corner,
a kind of farewell that
releases me to sleep.
until invisible. Gone, gone.

BIRD WORDS

House finches, pink-breasted,
sharp-beaked, pick at the black bird-seed
fallen from the feeder by our back door.

Further away, among the maple leaves,
other diminutive, unidentified birds flutter like
restless foliage.

Precise as Japanese cut paper, a leaf is also
a kind of feather. As if the tree's desire is
to take flight,

And in Fall, as the leaves leave, that wish
is fulfilled. I am myself a tree, my bird words
searching for branches to perch on,

to build nests,
lay eggs,
hatch chicks.

WHISPER

Clouds tear apart like bread broken,
and words scatter their crumbs

wherever they may attract a bevy of
precise, ready beaks.

Your story-telling voice speaks in a whisper.
Is this a secret? I ask.

No secret. Just an experiment in sound.
Were you listening?

LILIES OF THE VALLEY

Can fragrance shape
an image? Write a tune?
Leave a lasting
impression?

Like a nose,
my camera's lens,
eager, buries itself
for a close-up

of a minor startle of
white lilies
rising from the valley of
their green leaves.

A bell choir,
they stand there
in their little white caps,
planted by God,

who delights to listen
with us, to the music of
their fragrance.

MOVING THE DOGWOOD

Oh, you, whose twig-ends,
in the warming weather of April,
thicken by increments into
buds pregnant with promise.
You, who will open, under the Spring sun,
into a display of ruddy petals.
You, welcome as a member
of the family, planted as you were
on our corner where two streets
meet, you who were threatened by
machines large as elephants
that thundered down our hill, laying
concrete curbs like toothpaste
from a tube. Next, sidewalks,
installed where flowers flourished
all those years. But you, now dug up
and replanted closer to our house,
and therefore safe, our well-beloved
Cornus Kousa, may you know
unhindered happiness in your new
setting, you who annually spread for us
such garlands of rosy delight.

SCARLET

"Our red-berry-sour Kousa aflame . . ."
—Paul Mariani in *All that Will Be New*

How color speaks its name into the brain
against forgetting. And how it flourishes in
our veteran poet's words. How, in our own
front yard in Spring, the young *Cornus Kousa*
flaunted her brazen pinks destined to ripen into
Fall's blood-red berries, a bleed impossible to ignore.

Today, carving the roast for dinner,
my knife slipped, and bright blood trickled,
congealed, turned dark, and healed.

Ah, but what is a brief bleed compared to
the annual blaze of Dogwood blooms
ripening into blood-red berries?

JUST ADD WATER
(with apologies to Richard Powers)

The world is shaped for greening.
The mosses' unstoppable, slow surge
creeps across rocks, sprouts in every crevice,
consoling the eye with softness.

The maple's leaves open their fan-like,
five-fingered hands to catch today's bright
overtures of light.

Even on a still day,
aspens arouse their leaves as if in
an invisible wind.

Most of the forests we've witnessed,
across a smattering of seasons,
grow at the speed of wood.

As light sifts through the canopy,
slow and certain, their faerie arboreal systems
are being birthed into earth from the wide air
by a golden dust of spores.

In spite of our depredations
Their knowing branches subsist.

Linked with threads fine as gossamer
the charming shyness of their foliage
belies their unstoppable force.
Some communities of plants, willful and crafty,
plan to take over the world. Ignited by lightnings'
flaming airs, the words of fire consume the land,
rigorous as prophetic speech.

Who are we
to withstand this destruction?

How?

BREEZE

Under a brief breeze the little lake
shivers, then calms herself as if saying,
"I don't know what came over me!"

THE DANCE OF THE LICHENS

A damp day, and walking the woods, we discover them,
sprouting like miniature lettuces, spreading their
minor mantles, hoary and moist, curling at the edges—
lichens green and fine as human hair, decorating the rotten
stumps and rocks of the woodland, charming us by their
    pale
frills and baroque contours. You can't call them plants,
but they like to pretend. Claiming distant relationship
with fungi, macrolichens float into the air pale fibers
delicate as lace, a curious embroidery on the forests' face.

Enchanted, we photograph a dozen examples, some
fine as hair, some frilled as flower petals, pale, green,
gray, orange, dotted with red micro-spores, ready to fly,
to catch any minor air for conveyance, for symbiosis,
for claiming some damp environs as habitation.

Summer, and some, surviving the season's heat, creep
across bare rocks, enter granitic cracks, split
giant boulders by the persistent force of mere existence.

Today, on the path down to our creek, we saw them
    swarming,
dancing along the wooden handrail, balancing like
    gymnasts.

Variants of symbiosis, ambient, fanciful, buoyant, spotted, flaunting, frilled, flirting, feeding on the rot of forest floors, they decorate the underworld in gray-green, and gold.

EXUBERANCE, MT. BAKER
NATIONAL FOREST

Like a faded ribbon, the track unrolls through
the scrim of forest green, well-worn all year
by the faithful on their bicycles. But left and right,
the woods swell, swarming with life, sap rising, bushes
bursting, vigorous, verdant in the exuberant air.

In the grasses dew betrays multiple spider webs.
From every leaf light shines like a little sun.
Even the canes and brambles, after drinking rain
all winter, are leaping into the season. Green
gushes from every notch and knot, even from
the river reeds and the mosses on the rocks.

Standing there on the track, I drink in all that's
green and growing, every freshet, every pouring spring,
every drop a contestant in the season. My face
begins to glow with the reflected colors of
leaves. Even my feet want to take root in the loam.

DRIVING THROUGH THE SEASON

All day the summer roadside has offered its orisons
and expletives, glimpses of innocent buttercups, varnished
yellow, and fields white with tablecloths of Queen Anne's
Lace.
In a farmer's acreage two bay horses, grazing near the fence
in an unharvested field, nicker and amble over to see us.
Stretching west, acres of rattle box, yarrow, wild vetch, all
add up to a richly variegated landscape.

We acknowledge also, cursing under our breath, crab grass,
the toxic yellow star-thistle and cheat grass—weeds
we acknowledge with disapproval as the wet wipers swipe
the dusty windshield with streaky half-moons, as our tires
mutter their guttural syllables against the wet freeway.

We cross the Nooksack bridge, the river beneath us
brimming
almost at flood-stage, a declaration of warning at the outset
of a long rainy season. A highway mile or two further along,
under a silver slant of rain, an ancient barn leans at a
perilous angle, its broken siding leaking daylight,
garishly painted and spangled in red, white, and blue.

Come Fall, we anticipate the poplars and quaking aspens,
tricked out with gold leaf, will float their feathery blessings
down the still air, one faded riffle at a time, for our
   consolation.

Under weeks of rain the fields will flood again and the weeds
prevail. And we—we will drive north and back again.

Again. Surveying the land.

CROSSING THE CASCADES

Driving, we traverse
this massive mountain range,
this steep stumble of old,
dead rocks,

noticing the small
miracles of green,
the stabs of survival
in the most
improbable places.

Down one precipitous cliff
a single seed fell from its
mother cone and—*mirabile dictu*—
found a crack in the rock face
that welcomed entry.

Like a toenail
that catches and holds,
the root-ling thrust its
stab of life, its act of faith,
into the blind rock.

Its green life, by increments,
the reward for risk.

We pay passing attention
and our observation
turns it real.

LOOK UP

Those starlings,
that crowd of black wings
patterning the noon sky, flow
along a highway invisible,
unknown to us, we without
wings, stiff, anchored,
eyes on the rutted road
beneath our feet.

The risk of looking up,
is perhaps to lose our footing
in the enchantment of
cloud splendor, the stabs
of sunlight.

LAKE LIGHT

This little lake at the edge of the forest,
sunstruck and green-shadowed,
is absorbed, calm, admiring its own reflection
until the surface shivers, touched by
a little air, or maybe a fallen leaf.

Days like this glint when the light is right,
dilating the pupil of my attention.
I drink in the brightness like lemonade.

I remember how words inside me
can pierce my heart with loveliness,
an aching pain that discovers
its own music in a minor key,
only to give up with changing weather
re-tuning itself major.

THE APRICOT TREE
—Fall 2022
for Ben and Lisa

That afternoon, as I was
sitting in their sunny backyard,

the air's large hand
took hold of the apricot tree—

the one that had fruited
so bountifully, a lush yield

in late summer—
caught it in a downdraft of cool,

shook it lightly, again, again,
loosening each leaf

from its thumb of stem.
For two more days I watched the leaves'

pale drift ground-ward,
and, one by one, depart,

each crumpled flick of fiber
among all the glints of gold

an announcement, God saying,
gently, Thank you for your lovely life.

Now, time to let go.

WAITING FOR THE FERRY 1
Orcas Island, November 2021

We've allowed plenty of time.
From Eastsound we drive across the island
toward the ferry terminal; last night's rain
glitters in the drainage ditch roadside,
a river of mirrors—a map of light.

We wind ahead across farmers' fields
scanning for glowing leaves to satisfy
my eyes' hunger for Fall color.
We have plenty of time to notice how
this island landscape speaks, the shapes,
the colors forming words in my catchment mind.
How the trees show off their lovely bones!

We wait in the ferry line as foot travelers
stroll down to the terminal. Time stands still.
We have plenty of it for me to photograph
the green cushions of moss on the rocks,
and the madrones, their bark peeling,
showing warm tan on their motherly arms.

The "Samish" pulls into the dock.
Enough time, now, for the wide stretch
of glistening water to bless my eyes.

WAITING FOR THE FERRY 2
Orcas Island, October 2022

The line of cars, trucks, and a school bus winds
down the hill, with at least an hour's wait for
the ferry. For us it's bliss, this empty time,
this brief parenthesis of quiet within our lives.
An hour to dream and read, for John to sketch,
for me to scribble lines of verse, accompanied by
Bach, Mendelssohn, and Scarlatti in the car,
their inventions familiar, centuries old, but now,
new, perfect for waiting and reflection as the car's
close air is filled with the brilliant, gentle sound.

Across the road, a rock wall rises like a giant's
shoulder, its surface like a skin patterned with
a rough vegetable tattoo of blackberry vines. Fall's
days of dark and wet have chilled the leaves,
turning them pink, and cream, and a tender rose.
I am entranced, in love. Their leafy glowing
beckons me across the road, to harvest them with
the close focus of my camera's lens—these images
of autumn that speak to me of my own changing life.

NEW LEAF RESTAURANT

With the camera of my mind I try
to teach myself the view, anticipating
a destination before arrival, expecting
the benediction of weather, a warm sun
and a cool wind from the ocean, almost
believing my desire will bring it to pass.

Waiting has been always a discipline
alien to me. Yet I try to teach myself what
I need to know, to respond with gratitude
to guidance, perhaps salutatory,
yet offered with great generosity.

Wanting, as I wait, the message in the air
to be true, that when I arrive I may receive
with gratitude a friend's long-harvested
wisdom and discernment.

Impatience consumes me. Like a candle,
my dark wick of certainty burns down to
a lonely thumb of wax destined for snuffing,
its pale smoke drifting to the ceiling
like an angel's scarf, before vanishing.

Though I've been lonely, shorn of trust
and certainty, feeling bald and plain,
a friend's gracious green and gold
speech fills the untidy field of my belief
with new growth. Today all my living
spreads ahead of me, like a field in Fall
dank with wet, decorated with
wild flocks of white geese.

I love how, as I watch,
their congregation lifts and lowers
over the field, like a woman's white
sheets on a backyard line
raising their wings
in praise of the wide air.

CREEK-SIDE

We stroll the sidewalks of the planet,
the path's grassy shoulders
keeping us company

as we watch the water-falling
of the roadside creek
as it lays and layers the land.

Fall is coming too fast. The light
shifts, angling obliquely through the west-
facing windows of our lives

its sudden gold
glints its minor radiance on my
wide gold wedding band.

Four-thirty, and sundown already,
and we watch the slow, incoming
variations of evening, asking:

Why do tides obey
the pull of the moon, and the days
obey the sun?

There's always
a reason that reasoning
can only guess at.

WHALE

"Monday. The Port of Bellingham posted a photo of a visitor along Bellingham Bay. Humpback whales are commonly the size of buses."

—*The Bellingham Herald*, March 24, 2022

O mighty one, you whose bulky vehicle visits
our islanded western Sounds in early spring,
who, breaching, lift your mass in opulent suspension
above the waves, its grand re-entry flinging wide
a rainbow spray. You, whose magnitude now courses
along the continent's channel way, swimming
north to new, nutritious waters. You, leviathan,
astound us, a grandeur that causes godly fear
at your creation, and wonder at the deep sounding
of your uncanny songs. Whose fine baleen strains
from the waters a nutritious soup of krill,
the most minor of sea creatures nourishing the major.

May our fragmentary whispers of gratitude bless You,
the One among us who listens and, unearthly, speaks.

IN THE MIST

Fragrant with lilies,
along this minor road creeps a mist
so soft, silent, and capable
of dealing life
or sudden death.

Drive slowly.
Ease into the future as though
through a fog that drifts
like a spirit
over the lake at evening.

GINGKO LEAVES

Gingko leaves, with their double-lobed,
odd-shaped, somehow-alien foliage,
have been observed in Fall to fall all together
from their slender mother tree, a cloud of
golden flakes, all riffle and flick, flung
sideways by the wind—their lovely fan shapes
swirling down, settling, coming to rest
to coat some common, cracked pavement with
gold leaf until it forms a carpet as
splendid and exotic as a Gustav Klimt robe.

ONE LEAF, NOVEMBER

"All is leaf" —Goethe

That one, slightly scarred, tawny
tissue of life among thousands,
that one being held there on its mother tree
by a single sturdy finger of twig
ever since Spring. Varnished all summer
with sunlight, eating incandescence, its lumens
bodied under the cells' surface fabric.

Every day, driving into town, I'd notice
the leafy multitudes of glossy, perforated
leaves, each replica tethered on that one tree.

Until a single leaf fell, found itself pinned
by rain on my windshield. Tattered,
detached, adrift in the November wind,
and finally in a solo downward flight, its cells
its own, only, it will decay uniquely
among all the incomparable others.

THE STAR IN THE KITCHEN WINDOW

I was eager to believe that, hidden in her dusky
womb, this bud nurtures a vegetable impatience.
She'd arrived boxed, buried in a pot of dirt
and dry moss. I discover that her name,
"Amaryllis," means "sparkle," a designation
that ignites my own small spark of trust,
that urges me to believe that in this dry bulb
a diligent asterisk, a hidden wink of light
lives, waits, hopes, to grow and blossom.

In her pot I water her. I place her, saucered,
in a window for the light. I wait, curious.
When might this secret promise blossom
and burst into a star?

It's a lesson in patient faith. And waiting,
waiting. Did I mention waiting? A week.
Two weeks. Three, until a gleam, a bright thumb
of green thrusts up lowly from the dry dirt,
stretching up increments, lifting its compact,
complicated bud head until it bursts open
into a fine, white, five-petaled bloom.
Out of the pitiful earth, a star is born.

HOW LUCKY

we are to live in a country of bright wind and water,
where buoyant sails of clouds are carried along by
invisible hands.

The tulips, whose dark bulbs we planted last Fall, thrust
up their fierce, purple beaks, urging us to keep beauty alive.
A reminder: to be asleep is not to die but to wait faithfully.

The robins return every spring to take up their
sentry posts on the power lines, until the jays arrive
to disturb the peace.

The work crews arrive early, just as we wake,
playing with wet cement, laying it along the road's sides
into a curb, like bread dough to be kneaded and baked.

The weekly garbage trucks arrive also, to deal with
our profligate abundance, the well-worn
and the casual cast-offs.

So lucky we are to live where along our street
the ancient trees robe themselves in emerald moss,
where the ferns color the air green.

Lucky, meaning *blessed,* a state we achieve not
through labor, but by observing with clarity this very day.
This God-blessed, lucky day.

SATURDAY AFTERNOON,
WAITING FOR THE MAIL

The mail van is visible
up the street. I can just
see it.

The mail carrier
is leaning out of her little van,
planting mail in
the neighborhood boxes.

Her window
is open at
just the right level.

It is like sowing seed.

I clamber across our street,
up the curb, mailbox
key in hand, and wait.
I love the mystery. What is it
that will show up in the secret
envelopes bearing
my address?

My neighbor's yard is
close by. As I wait
I pluck the plume grass from
his neighbor's nearby rock garden,

its tall stalks and feathery heads
perfect for Fall
flower arrangements.

And, just a few feet
further in, yellow daisies.

I ask you,
what better thing is there to do
on a Saturday afternoon
than to gather grasses with
feathery heads,

and yellow daisies,
to celebrate summer
as we fall
into Fall.

KNITTING IN THE WILD
Douglas Fir campground, August 2022

I sit by the tent, knitting a jacket.
Below the bank, the Nooksack's green
rush of water never goes quiet,
blankets all other sounds.

A thin, jade river of yarn rises
to my needles from the ball in the bag,
the alpaca soft in my fingers.
Knit and purl, I coax a pattern onto
the yellow needles.

It will be very beautiful.
Buttonholes will march up
the front, spaced as judiciously
as line breaks in a poem.

Row upon row, word after word,
in my journal I pencil them in,
knitting nouns and verbs together until they
click into place,

until a more fluid image arrives,
desiring to grow into a poem.
Or at least, a new green jacket
for a friend.

IN A FIELD

The trees stand like ancient prophets—
one, and another, in a field full of sheep,

and one more, a few yards further along,
where the fence opens its gate

onto the dirt road. Each tree,
singly and solemnly, waits,

expecting the sun to come out any moment
to read its multiple leaves

like pages in a book of poems whose lines
I feel called to study, hoping for

a brief enlightenment, but where
intricacies of foliage read only

like scathing comments about the foolish
farmhand who left the gate open.

And now the sheep are escaping,
as was to be expected.

ABOVE TAOS GORGE

We drive out of the town,
and park on the high bridge
above the gorge.

From the sidewalk
we peer over the edge.

Below, in a deep cleft in the earth,
a stream glistens.

It is like
opening a vein,
It is that deep.

Across the bridge,
a sidewalk artisan
is selling stones to tourists.

I cross the road, ask
to see. He chooses one, puts
it in the palm of my hand.

It is a polished black,
the size of a muffin.
It is heavy and warm
from the New Mexico sun.

Across its dark surface
runs a crack like
a thready river,
into which the artist
has pounded shards
of turquoise.

And the stone? I claim it, buy it, carry it home,
for visitation and remembrance.

UNIVERSE
UNI -VERSUS, TOGETHER TURNING AROUND

He drives and the highway un-spools under our tires.
I knit—stitch, and stitch—my yarn un-spooling
from its skein onto my needles, turning at the end of
each row. The way we're driven to circle round
at a dead end and search for a different destination.
The way our planet moves, turns, revolves, tilts,
maintains its course within the universe.

So, we're heading west, a direction that summons us
into its light at high noon. A mile or two, and there's
an exit for a side road. We turn into it, arriving soon
at a locked iron gate and the hindering sign—Dead End,
posted in red on a rusted metal plate. Entrance denied.

Yet it's right there, in the place of disappointment,
that sunlight winks its enchantment off the weeds
thrusting up among clutters of broken stones. There we
park, with a blue glimpse of the bay, content, unobserved,
settled in comfort. On the car radio, Mendelssohn
and Bach. John reads *The Christian Century.* I work on
this poem in my journal, and the radiance of the day
is sustained by the God of the circling universe.

II

~

WEATHERING

CICADA NIGHT

A warm cicada night. The thrum of insects
wipes out the sounds of traffic, bird calls, children's
voices. Then, like a warm weather front,
a swarm of syllables, words that have sucked the juice
from the roots of language, begins to gather
on my journal page. Sometimes, like spent insects,
the fragments fall on dry ground, leaving only
delicate patterns of damp, transparent wings.

A long day, generously blue, and then
clouds, a shy rain, and the soft perfection of dusk.
Wet leaves and the lenses of raindrops magnify
the blemishes that are minor, and forgivable.

I need to be there, like a news reporter, with a new,
clean page in my notebook, open like a glass jar,
to gather from underfoot the evening's
hot, crunchy, language.

FRESH

From the sun-ghosted roadside grass
voices of light speak.

Listen. Then, enlivened,
keep walking until
you come to a fast-flowing stream.

Take off your shoes, and step into
the force and flow of its chill
until it numbs your flesh
and tingles your spirit.

WAITING FOR WORDS

I want the words, all
lined up, to feel like children waiting
to run outside to recess.

Sprung tight, restless—
nouns, verbs, adjectives seem barely restrained
in their enthusiasm for freedom,
eager for wide open space, for far blue air,
they gear up, prepared to leap onto
the page with ease and without hesitation.

Listen now for children's voices—shouting,
screaming, whooping, singing in the happy sun—
they all coalesce in a kind of orchestral sound:
largo, presto, agitato, and a few minutes later,
with distance, diminuendo.

HOW IT HAPPENS

When the words begin to arrive in my mind,
like tourists with cameras primed for the views,
they show up to be introduced. Yesterday they
arrived late morning, bringing with them
bunches of exotic wildflowers and birds
with songs like bells ringing. For snacks, they
unpacked fragrant fruit to be nibbled
under the jacaranda trees. I inhaled their syllables'
soft breath, allowing them time to simmer into
some crisp internal identity, some fresh, surprising
sound or color. The words arrive visible,
like dandelion seeds that speak themselves into the air...
Then, surprise, a fresh phrase shows up,
tingling, excited to be invited, welcomed to
the party. I begin to sense the phrases thinking back
at me, *thinking me* in a sweet, internal colloquy—
interested in how our words sound
when spoken together into the bright air.
This is how my mind disputes amicably with
itself, one of the ways creation happens.
How freshness breaks in. How a new, crunchy
poem can begin, impatient, demanding to be
written down. And that is how a poem happens.

STONES

Writing, the words wait in line,
a row of polished stones

ready to be skipped across the lake.
That is their desire as well.

Though, if I am clumsy, my flung words—
gravelly, jagged—will sink like rocks.

Better, I'll fling a fistful of
seeds, words bursting from a ripe pod,

believing the wind will find for them
a soil rich enough to grow in,

to send up buds, flowers. Their meaning
will hang in the air—waiting for
a light breeze.

SUDDEN

for Karen Cooper

Out shopping in the supermarket
you overhear an intriguing
conversation,
maybe a phrase that stumbles,
uninvited,
into your ear,
demands your attention.

You can't help but
pencil the words
on the back of the crumpled envelope
you find in your purse.

Later, the random phrases
unfold themselves until they lie
naked on the page.
A chance poem, it tells itself
back to you,
curious.

Later, you'll call your friend in Canada
to read it over the phone.
She will undoubtedly suggest
revisions that sound,
in your grateful ear,
just right.

LAUNDRY LIST

With a whole lexicon of intriguing language available
to make a poem, images and words churn like clothes
in the dryer, like wrinkled sheets hung in the sun, as strong
    air
smooths the crumpled fabric.

Sixty years back, and I remember drying laundry
in our backyard. I'd pin damp dish towels
and bright shirts to wires strung with stiff wooden pegs,
fabric gleaming, ballooning in air spacious as imagination.
Think a row of socks, like commas, colons. Think
a colloquy of dresses, lambent words, rhythms and rhymes
glowing at noon, ready for the poet-mind to pluck and
    show—
their primary colors, the gleaming fabric of metaphors,
all embracing the wind's incoming tide like ships under full
    sail.
At the approach of rain, I'd clutch them for the laundry
    basket.
Like catching the drift of a metaphor floating in the birthing
wind. Like fresh-folding words into a new poem.

WOMAN IN BLUE

In *Woman in Blue Reading a Letter*,
Vermeer shows us a quiet, Dutch interior,
inviting us to peer into the tranquil
domestic scene to see a woman in profile.
She is standing, generously dressed in calm
blues and grays. She is reading a letter.
From where we stand, peering in, we see
the letter but not the words it holds.
We note the indirect light that bathes the interior,
but not the window through which the light
is pouring. Our entry into the painting
is so much guesswork. Though the scene is calm
and lovely, it challenges us, if we are honest.
The artist nudges us to move beyond
surfaces, to observe detail, to analyze composition,
to examine his art with intention. Quietly, indirectly,
he teaches us how to see. Isn't this also
how a poem works? Too easy
to interpret in one reading, it can be a trifle glaring,
even tedious. For the writer to explain detail
may deprive us of the pleasure of our own
gratifying, investigative work, work that demands
close attention, that will pull us into the center of
the work until we appreciate what a gift is Vermeer's art.

NEW POEM

You open your journal to a fresh, clean page,
an open space for crisp words to speak themselves
into a smart, original poem. You wait, then, for the
best nouns and verbs to show up. It is like waiting
for new neighbors to come over and introduce
themselves, you hoping they come to
the front door, all eager and friendly, offering a
freshly baked blueberry pie, wanting to tell you how
much they like your landscaping, and can you
recommend a good gardener?
So, that's your page, offering itself to you
for good or ill. You write your clever poem
onto it, the poem that is your life, good for sharing.

SO MUCH DEPENDS

How the written words jostle each other, black insects
creeping across the notebook page! How the esoteric
symbols join, re-telling your story as they stumble
along the lines, black against white. There's a whole
narrative there, a story wanting to be told. You modify it
as you go, your eyes guiding your mind gently, traveling
left to right across the well-worn playgrounds of page and
    screen.
Your thoughts unfold themselves raggedly, disrobing
by increments until they lie naked on the page.

Then, a character you hadn't intended introduces herself,
requiring special attention. You give in to her, as you do
to other details as they crowd the narrative. You re-read
the rough draft, and a tempting leap of your imagination
finds a plotline that seems to pull it all together.

Later, though, when you test it, reading the words aloud,
the story tastes unready, raw on the tongue. Actions
move the story along briskly, but a metaphor, meant
to enrich the plot, is still unfocused—a blur to be either
clarified or abandoned.

You speak the words into the listening air, needing
to hear them aloud, hoping for them to come together
cleanly, for the verbal mix to carry its own logic,
for your inventive strategy to add up. And as the story line
thickens, characters settle in for the long run, actions
growing coherent, making sense. So much depends…

SEQUOIA

Sometimes I'll drop an unmanageable poem
onto paper delicate as a moth wing, a tissue
that threatens to crumble
at the slightest touch.

I've wondered about writing on bark,
perhaps the gnarly outer garment of a sequoia
that has lived its years—a thousand
or more—a giant thick as God's arm,
as it reaches up through the overstory.

Then, should the ultimate wildfire eat out
the heart of the grove, my words will
go up to God in flames.

WEATHERING

A long day, profligate with rain,
followed by a crystalline night and
a prodigality of stars.
Such a spendthrift God we have

who gave us all this! Who also
spread, with his large hand, rosy
streaks of light over this morning's
cloud heaven and hilltop!

Doesn't your breath sometimes quicken
at such magnificence, like a wave
cresting? And then, the astonishment
that you can tell it out, can share it

with your good friends, generous
as sunlight through the golden maples,
gorgeous as the golden gleam
of the wedding ring on your finger.

How else can you hold all the world-
loveliness but by pinning it in print on paper,
then, feasting on it, free of charge,
in the holy company of poet friends?

DECEMBER

Last night I lay awake and practiced
getting old. Painful, but not difficult.

I needed to teach myself to love my destination
before I arrive.

As time stretches ahead I feel the earth shift
and my writing hand shakes—its nudges

stretching, rubbery, weak, the way a day
will lose its light and give itself to darkness,

and that long, inquisitive pause—
What next? And how long before

light reopens her blue eye? I am one who waits,
still, to arrive

where language breeds, unhindered.
There I can dip into the depths of words,

inhale their profound syllables, and
live there a long time, with relief and enjoyment,

and never need to come up
to breathe.

III

~

THE FALL TO
EARTH

MARY AND THE ANGEL

How often we've heard how Gabriel,
God's messenger, brings to young Mary
    astonishing news.

This time we follow the Angel
through the open doorway into Mary's room.
    We hear his greeting, "The Lord is with you!"

"What can this mean?"
Mary wonders.
    We wonder too.

Then, astonishment: The Angel announces that God
has chosen her, this little, virgin girl,
    to bear a boy baby for God!

We're close enough to hear her
gasp and breathe her astonishment. Then,
    her utterly reasonable inquiry, "But, how?"

But when Gabriel invites her into
God's plan to enter the world, within her,
    through her,
    we hear her whisper, "*Yes!*"

And with her simple consent
we feel the universe shift. Grow new.
Will never be the same.

THE HOPE OF GLORY

Months later, with the seed of God
rounding her belly with promise,
I wonder, was Mary restless in the night,
her back aching, soft stirrings
waking her from slumber?

Elizabeth understood,
and when the two got together
and the cousins in their wombs leaped
toward each other, quivering
with recognition, what hopes,
what dreams did the two women share?
Did they guess how the story would end,
for their sons, for us?

And we, young as Mary, old as Elizabeth,
woman or man, do we not each long to feel
the seed of God shifting within us,
a guarantee of now and future
life and glory?

SNOW

With what calm and gentle grace
last night's fresh poem of snow
was laid across the land, whitening the hills,
filling the simple spaces between
the birches. Fallen snow is an easy essay
in quietude, in anonymity. And when
the Baby came—He who carved
those hills, who designed each lacy branch
on every tree, who shaped that
gleaming signal star borne from high heaven—
it was He whose splendor fell to earth,
so simply, quietly as a flake of snow,
to bring to all our troubled, broken world
his gifts of grace and beauty.

MARY'S SWORD

On the Feast of the Baptism of the Lord

"Yes, and a sword will pierce your own heart also..."
—Luke 2:35

The fortieth day, and now we watch as
the little family waits in the temple
for old Simeon to bless the new Baby.

Listen, and hear then, his prophetic declaration:
one of promise and import for the human race—
our ascending, our decline. Then, quite shockingly,
he tells young Mary, her infant in her arms,
"...Also, a sword will pierce your own heart."

Hearing that warning, does she suck in her breath?
And that foreboding thrust—will it haunt her,
living as she must, on the fringes of her Son's
too-brief life? When others leap up, restored
by his touch, might not her own heart's flesh knit,
its raw edges scarring over?

But we guess that Mary lived the weapon's threat
through all the years until its deepest wound, when,
witness of her Son's harsh dying, the spear-thrust in his side
assured her of a healing, and a resurrected life.

And on that day of darkness, could she have known
that all our generations would rise
and call her blessed?

A CHILD'S QUESTIONS

Jesus, that little tyke with the curly hair,
still just a happy-go-lucky kid—this youngster
on the cracked tile floor, playing with
the cedar shavings that fall in fragrant curls
from his daddy's plane—did he dream his life
shifting ahead into a new identity? To be one
who called his friends to get up, and leave
their ordinary human lives to follow him? Perhaps
his urgent human body always carried a visionary
spirit, listening to the call, the challenge to love
the wider world he'd brought into being

Watch, now, the child's eagerness to learn
the family business! As he listens for Joseph's
hammer blows, the lilt of lathe, the thrust
of iron nails into wood, does he begin to love
those lively rhythms of creation and construction?
And growing up, did he wonder if he himself
might simply come to wear a workman's leather apron,
dreaming of becoming a master carpenter?

Or did he always heed that higher destiny,
in which another artifact of wood and nails is raised
to hold his body high, announcing to the world
his own intent to mend its brokenness?

SCANT

What balance
may be found between
profit and loss? Is there ever
a fitting reward for
endurance?

Make that personal;
may I feed on scarcity
as Jesus did, subsisting forty days
in the wild, on stones, the scourge
of the Spirit, the predations
of the accuser, the intent
of the Father?

Can the dryness—what is scant
and spare—be wrung out
to yield some more nourishing
essence?

We count on the
nutriments in bone broth.
Bodies are one thing,
but the soul also has a structure
that pleads for survival.

We discover this
only *in extremis*.
Waiting there, longing
for the indispensable
to meet our deep need.

JESUS TELLS HIS STORY

I have nothing.
I hope only for the love of my friends.
They make all this talk of
following me,

yet they worry more about
paying off the mortgage,
selling the fresh catch of fish
before they begin to rot,
and meeting friends at the pub tonight.

My talk of riches in heaven
makes little sense to them.
What they really want from me
are reservations in paradise
and the best seats
close to the throne.
All their talk of following me—
of loving me,
of being faithful...

Most nights, while they
go home to their own beds
and their warm wives,

I'm left wondering, *Where will I sleep?*
(The ground is stony and the wind
gusts even colder after dark.)

And when hunger grips me,
what crusts of day-old bread
Might I find at the bakery
on the outskirts of town?

My Father knows all this,
tells me once again of the
wonderful plans he's been making
ever since the world's foundation....

Yet he's still asking of me this one,
final thing (as the space between us widens
the closer I get to Jerusalem).

Of course, I could change all this
with a word. I could make
other arrangements....

IV

~

ENERGY &
ENTROPY

ENERGY & ENTROPY

Energy, a consistency of effort,
mind and muscle reaching
for option, action, engagement.

The tulip bud flowering into flame.
Flush, fresh, living.

Entropy, an attenuation, then,
as hours pass into days
with their fatigue,
the iridescent petals shrinking,
sinking, drooping, dropping,
color draining, dying.

Pair the antonyms,
energy and entropy,
unusual partners
twinned in the making of love,
to join with all the unmaking
and remaking within
the fluid universe.

TO DO

Miss phone call.

Lose phone.

Find phone.

Lose phone again.

Look under desk.

Finally find phone.

Make phone call.

Line busy.

Confuse dates.

Miss appointment.

Misfile documents.

Make lists.

Lose lists.

Write letter.

Mislay address book.

Lack stamps.

Drive to Post Office.

Closed.

Drive to Bank. Also closed.

Deposit check in ATM.

Need withdrawal.

Lose bank card

Drive home in rain.

Drink merlot.

Empty wine bottle.

Lose mind.

OLDER

Aging haunts, will hunt us all, a predator,
rapacious, ravenous, toothed with sharp anxieties.
The scars of old and unhealed wounds hide
in the folds of soul skin. Blood stains the ground.
Failures, regrets have left torn tissues,
ragged blemishes and a crimson trail
across the room. You feel it wet, sticky, seeping
between your bare toes. In the thick night,
You wrestle with dreams, contend with confusion.

How good it would be if the anxiety of aging,
bulky and useless, were a piece of furniture.
You might remove it from the living room and
store it somewhere dark, out of sight—
in the basement, perhaps, locked behind
the cellar door. Then you could climb back up to
the clean kitchen, a room predictable enough
to allay suspicion. You'd open a window,
maybe prepare a simple meal. Pray.

TRACK

Entering the deep forest of age and anxiety
along the dark track that leads to unexplored
territory, I bring a flashlight. It flickers
its faint light on the trail ahead. Sometimes, though,
I turn off the little beam to feel the dark
at its deepest, hoping the path doesn't lead to
a blind end, doesn't peter out. Under my feet I feel
soft bark and pine needles. And further on, gravel,
sharp pebbles, tree roots, rotting bark. I stumble,
recover, stumble again until I emerge on
a sun-drenched river bank. I listen to the shallow
chatter of water as it tumbles over a pebbled
stream bed. As it moves away between its
weedy banks I listen for its friendly mutter still.
Its water music.

OUT WALKING

The righteous one will flourish like a green tree,
growing like a cedar in Lebanon ... in old age
always green and full of sap. —Psalm 92:12–14

They show up in the X-rays, my old knees
stiff and clumsy but still steadfast under me,
the metallic implants like trusty locks that no key
can open. And my left leg, with its three-times-
broken ankle, shored up with a brace of
plastic, metal, and Velcro. I sometimes wonder
how to live like the cedar tree in the psalm,
whose thickened, ancient branches and roots
are designed by God to persist, green
and full of sap into old age. This afternoon,
John and I will fold my walker, stow it in the trunk,
and go out driving. Deep in the woods, we'll
slow down, open the car window, and let the deep
woodland wash over us, breathe into us,
the trees reminding us of their slow green and
certain growth. Then, with the walker, I'll lurch
along a few yards on a forest path, encouraged
and renewed by its natural beauty.

ISLAND, SPRING 2022

Like a knife through a flat calm the ferry cuts across
to the island. Jewels strung along the coast,
the snowy mountains to the north cast glistening
mirror images on the water's face. You land on Lummi,
drive the gentle coast road going west.

A fresh April green laces every tree, every weed.
You park on the gravel. In the bushes you find the thin,
hidden thread of track that leads down to the right.
You cannot see the shore, or the edge of the beach.
Yet. But you have confidence in the path, like
knowing a poem from memory. You wonder, ninety-four,
with shaky legs, your trouble with balance.... But you
tap into your venturing spirit and begin your stumble
down over knotty roots, your feet feeling for footholds,
blackberry thorns catching at your jacket.

There's the sweet smell of crushed foliage. Threads
of sunlight begin to show you the beached, bleached,
storm-tossed logs, the old bones of massive trees lying
helter-skelter on the shore. You crunch across the expanse
of beach. At the water's edge, lips of gleam kiss the pebbles.
Now and then, a glint of sea glass, but an infinite spread
of slate and agates and schist and red brick fragments

worn sleek as satin, and all the lapidary stones in the sun
call you. You pocket two or three smooth, water-worn gems,
clues to re-membering the benediction of beauty you will
ferry back with you to the gray mainland.

SURPRISE

Spring is always an astonishment. You'd think
by now we'd know what to expect, after all our
decades of year in, year out. We're surprised
that it's so surprising, so soul-gladdening,
this God-gift of a waking, warming season.

It's as if we've forgotten, or never noticed,
the how and why of Eastertide, when, like our
fasting souls, the dry sticks and stalks of winter
begin again to flesh out, succulent, drinking in
heaven's gift of silver rain. Growing green—
the astonishment of it! As if we're once again
jubilant in the arousal, the flush and flash of
wind gusts hitting the windows with wet kisses,
like birth announcements. How welcome, this
strong weather, this God-gift that knocks off
the scabs of our old winter, leaving us new,
new, eager to give praise for heavenly mercies
as announced in the daily forecast.

Now, ring every bell you own! Be noisily glad,
raising the roof! Now, do it again! Never tire of
giving God our jubilant thanks!

GRACE

Grace comes in every
gather of green, burgeoning forth
at trivial intervals, arriving
in an unexpected,
welcomed, burst.

Grace from heaven
animates, brings gratitude for green
shade in the summer swelter,
easing the burn of the sun's thick, hot
tongue, its insatiable lick on
your weathered traveler's brow.

In the desert, any least blade
offered—of shade, cool leaf, vine, or
scented bright bloom—is an act of
loving kindness.

In the fields, in a stalk of cane,
a sweet juice flows to rinse
the dry soul with the fresh taste
of grace.

LEVEL

How to test the quality of a plan,
a life? How to erect a structure
firm enough to stand on? Build on?
Work from? Rest in? You need

something like the carpenter's
cool, metal level to shift back
and forth in your hands, adjusting
with careful movements—up, down,
nudging the clear bubble of air
until it rests, centered, looking at you
like God's watchful eye.

Get to work, then, confident,
your resolve firm enough to build,
without fear, a house in which God's people
may gather. A house that welcomes God
with open arms. A house that God
may gladly enter, live in, bless.

ENLIGHTENED

The impression of an impression—
a cloud like the wing of a heron,
but blurred, and in ten minutes shape-
changed. This is how data reach us
from beyond, seductive,
indistinct, imprecise.

Yet determined to understand,
we study and discuss until we think
we've reached a conclusion, something
steady enough to stand on. Until
reason collapses like a broken
bridge, inadequate.

How clouds obscure the sky! How
we stumble our way through the darkened
woods, following a path tangled with roots
and incoherence until, almost by accident,
we arrive by the lake, and the moon's doubled
image drowns us in soft light.

V

~

LOVE IN THE TIME OF PLAGUE

BRASS TRAY

Before my birth, before I was even a gleam
in my parents' plan for life, my father's restless spirit
urged my mother to travel the world.

Nearly one hundred years ago, and now the wide
brass tray they brought back from North Africa,
incised all over with circles, with patterns like
flowers, like leaves, like secret, sacred symbols—waits
on its wooden stand by our west-facing window.

For too long I had ignored it, paid it scant attention,
but today I noticed how, as it waited through
the winter months, a smatter of dust and tarnish had dulled
its glory, and the bright, lovely metal needed
to be coaxed back into its essential glow and gleam.

So now, late afternoon, after my strenuous effort
with soft cloths and gray polish, it sits, an indoor sun,
beaming, ablaze, reflecting western afternoon light, an essay
in how beauty will not be always dimmed, no matter
how long it waits.

FLIGHT

after Rowan Williams

I was seven, alone in a house with adults who
seemed ancient. Restless, I was ready for any green
venture. Blood throbbing in young arteries, I fled
the house's suffocation and escaped into the bright
and generous air beyond the cloakroom, beyond
the back door, beyond all the dull internments.

Shaped by bright, occasional clouds, a whole
world waited, a spread of green, colored free
with robins, wrens, other unlabeled birds who find
a distance farther than their own feathered nests.

There, later, I grew my own set of wings, my mind
flown into a new geography where thoughts might
speak in newly developed languages, and ideas nest,
secure in spaces without lines, dressed in unmanageable
colors too bright to translate, too buoyant to hold down.

WHAT TO ADMIRE

The way a still lake esteems its own tranquility,
and how a breeze encourages the lily pads
to slide on the surface in new configurations.

An emerging poem adventurous enough to ignore
the lines in my journal, trespassing across
the page, leaping over onto the opposite other side.

A camera lens that cannot resist the dewy green
of leaves caught between early light
and morning fog.

A heart friend eager to climb
the mountain range of years with enthusiasm.

And another, who meets life the way a plow
meets the soil, turning it up to examine
what still lives beneath.

PRIMEVAL

Breathing cool syllables of early air, I admit I've never
been this old before. I amble through this fresh day,
halting often, avoiding the roots of huge oaks
that have cracked the sidewalk. They are ancient,
muscular, older even than I am.

And now, coming to meet me, there you are,
my friend, younger, energetic as a weed, breathing
your own algorithm of vigor into our shared atmosphere.

Walking together, we converse in well-worn,
familiar words to acknowledge the day: that early bird,
as he sings his wake-up song, and how jewel dew
reveals the art of spiders in the grasses.

And now, look! A bench for an intermission! I love
sitting there with you, under these leafy tree umbrellas,
letting the forest comfort us. In the perfectly still, chill air,
a single leaf falls at our feet, a delicate crumple
of color on the ground.

The day is too early to be warm. Yet of a sudden we
look up and you are, pointing, astonished, as the sky in the
East

breaks open with the fervent color of a pomegranate.
I wonder whether, later, I'll even remember to remember
how in this moment, everything comes together, in
a perfection that renews itself daily.

RESPONSES

In this poem, I hope to hear
your heartbeat
and your breathing, double
gears meshing smoothly.

In a letter you say you want
to sense my body on the paper—
its fevers, its failures,

creating an arterial
music, gestures
unique to us both, that echo,
each to each.

Our mutual response—
your heart fluid pulsing
in my arteries. My thinking
sparking yours.

HEARTWOOD
The Song of the Spoon-carver

There in the deep vastness of wilderness,
the great maple stands, thriving, enlarging
by increments over the centuries, waiting, all
the while, for recognition as its cells sing their
silent song. Xylem and phloem, resin and sap
in its slow heart wait, have waited, expectant
for centuries. And the Ancient One, He who
planned the seed, who first formed it, dropped it
on the floor of the forest, who tended its rooting,
its pushing up, burgeoning, growing in majesty.
He who watched its woody trunk broaden,
toughen, enlarge through drink and drought—
who envisioned its leafy glory, who also foresaw
its crashing downfall at the hands of men. He
who predicted its shaping with saws, its milling
and marking—it is he who holds it now, for
a human whittler's excavation of the sappy maple
heart, in which a spoon-shaped twist of woody
sinew waited to be revealed. Until now. So,
today, the woody spoon, rescued and carved
with loving care, offers itself, its unique curvature,
for stain and oil. Use it now, to scoop jam
or honey from a jar and taste the wildness
of centuries on the tip of your tongue.

LOVE IN THE TIME OF PLAGUE

You. Yes, you who have survived, have resisted
the invasion of the plague, whose face, familiar,
though masked, still smiles, the skin around your eyes
wrinkling with such genuine affection that no mask can
conceal the relief, disrupt the warmth of our being
together—you've arrived. I happily engage in rich converse
with you, trusted companion, a match striking, a lit wick
sending its petal of flame to flood our dark lives
with unguarded tenderness. Today, then, let us celebrate
friendship that no thick fabric can conceal, no distancing
prevent. When you finally arrive through the front door
I'll wait for the unmasking, the slow reveal, your face
saying everything without speaking a word. Like a door
opening, or a morning window, may love move freely
within our living room, taking the old chair by the fireplace,
stroking the warm fur of the rescue cat.

UP CLOSE

On these days made up of caution and dismay
I miss the particularity of your face, its features
seen up close, unguarded, the rhythm of your breathing
steady in my ear, your expression not hidden
behind the double mask of caution and necessity.

Every day, lately, I've longed for the quiet
reveal, the clear expression as your mouth moves
with words of love. To recognize in your
unguarded face the curl of amusement at a
private joke, your eyes speaking without words.

How to break through the devices we wear
for protection? To speak cleanly into the air
without contagion, our words following
the well-known tracks of connection,
of understanding that comes of long-held affection?

We've learned to count on a galaxy of tenacious
truths that lie under the skin, that no distance
will interrupt, that will not fade like breath on a
mirror, that no double mask can disrupt.

INTERMISSION

My memory gathers fragments of
the old past, recollecting flood, and storm,
but also the startling blue of delphiniums and
the rosy breast feathers of the house finch.
How together we discovered the hidden
geometry of rocks. Now, it all shows up
for me to recognize and remember.

Perhaps we both hope for a brief caesura,
a halt in the heart of the season for remembering
and recollection? We might begin by unfolding
old images, perhaps reading them like the pages
of a book, and hoping for maybe a single,
tranquil moment to live them again?

Yesterday I needed to know why
something painful had happened between us,
so we could put it to rest, move on,
perceive the future beautiful, untarnished.

Together, then, we may be able to make sense
of our lives, holding them, all and everything,
secure in the small jewel boxes of recollection
and forgiveness. Whether in fog or flake

the sky is falling, even as sunlight speaks its
pale encouragement through a break in the cloud.

Like a door opening, you will wait for light,
or a high window. From somewhere
a bowl of illumination is about to break open,
to spill over us both, never to dissolve.

VI

~

FINAL BREATH

REMEMBERING ROSALIND

Rosalind Young Deck
December 2022

The family meal that Jen had assembled when I was
in town, a genial gathering, jokes, lively conversations—
Muskoka's record snow, downtown traffic, new Scrabble
     words—
so much nimble repartee and laughter and good will among
three generations of Decks around the dinner table,
mutual affection among us spilling richly as the turkey gravy.

All the while, among your children and grandchildren
you sat, mute and unhappy. Later, as we drove you home,
your old resentments flaring—bitterness for my brother
     John,
the divorce, a catalog of his flaws and failings, a litany of
your disappointments. I asked about your knitting, and did
     you
use the yarn we'd chosen together, a pale gray the color of
this evening's rain-spattered car windows. Still the caustic
memories, the hurts you could never let go, never forgive.

Now your old woman body lies at rest in Jen's soft bed,
stuffed animals under your dead fingers for comfort, your
    face
in the final photographs slack and lifeless, your nails
    polished
a vivid pink.

In memory of my brother, John Henry Northcote Deck
1932–2022

1

LEAVING

How dutifully Fall's coppery leaves
layered themselves, the earlier fallen having
spread a first carpet over the dry rug of gravel
and October grass. Steep hillsides are flushed
with ruddy foliage, the leaves on the vine maples
preaching how senescence may be a lovely thing.

Yet I cry about the losses, the inevitable decay,
the leaving and dying, praying with small remaining
fragments of memory, for my family loves, for soul
friendships (I buff memories the way I polish
my ancient wooden writing desk with soft cloth
until it gleams, smelling of furniture wax).

May what is yet to come, to be borne in memory,
be, at least for now, sustained. Here, in this moment,
I yearn to learn the inner discipline of seeing
something treasured like loving, like fraternal kinship,
watching it moving away, relinquishing it, then
letting it go. Letting it go.

2

FINAL BREATH

My nephew held the phone close
to his dad's ear. His father—my brother, John,
near death in a Quebec hospital bed.

Close enough—I wanted to believe it—
for him to hear my words of loving farewell,
though how could I be sure that he knew they
were mine? Close enough for me to hear his
one long, faint, final breath.

Ninety years of highs and lows. Gasps,
fueled by drugs, inhalants, flaws tempered
by regrets. The car accidents, the broken glasses,
the brief relief of unconsciousness, the shattered
relationships, the promises of abstinence,
the failures and denials, the remorse.

Yet how proud I was of him, of all the academic honors,
the international lectureships, the visiting professorships,
the vast collection of microscope slides
exhibiting the varied pathologies of the human brain.
(He literally wrote the textbook.)

In our teens, our sibling lives were lived in parallel.
Camping, sailing, swimming, canoeing, island and shoreline
—all the love of rock and water. The two of us the only ones
who'd known and cared for each other from the beginning.

Always I'd had high hopes for John, for a reversal that might
dig deeper than mere regret. There were the new resolutions,
and we'd all be happy about some new start, knowing,
from experience, that it would not last.

3

THE SIFT OF GRIEF

How granular are grief and sorrow, arriving
in the particularities of distress, like sharp
pebbles in your shoe. How cunning and intricate,
as a species of panic ensues, bearing down the hours.

Impossible to ignore.

In the long night, grievances multiply.
Disappointment, doubt, and regret bludgeon the soul.
Your best dreams show up bruised, your hopes ragged.

Yet look—from the skylight the room fills with soft
early sun, its fine motes, welcome, reliable. They sift
across the bed, blessing your dead, peaceful face.

4

ON THE DEATH OF MY BROTHER
—Aged 90 on the day of his dying

I wait, and wait, wondering how long it will take
for final sorrow to unfold. For grief to crest and ebb.
And asking for what needs, still, to be felt to the core,
to be experienced, and its pain breathed into the air.

My brother, my only sibling, has just died, old and
disheartened, lonely, though surrounded by descendants,
having reached high, and succeeded, and failed.
Failed, despite achievement upon achievement.

How to move on, now, through the fog of sadness,
its silence, its finality, without drowning in desolation?
The chill of loss extends to my fingers' tips.
To breathe in sorrow is to inhale darkness with a hint of
        smoke,
a foretaste of my own mortality, a remembrance
of ashes on the forehead.

Lord, have mercy.

5

AFTERMATH

The time it takes for the mind to count the sum
of sorrow is like the slow reading of a creased letter
in faded ink. Memories flicker, images flashing
of a brother's aging face, flecked by sunlight,
fading like clots of ash. Reading, and re-reading
the words, and then, reading them now with you,
ushers a kind of acquiescence into grief.

Telling aloud the jagged narrative of a life,
in words that freely speak their pain, gives me time
and space to swallow death's cold meal,
a repast still flavored with bitter herbs.

I count on time to let sun and shadow shift
onto the page—regret, gladness, damage, love,
a narrative of adversity and fatigue followed by
merciful recall and relief.

6

THE BOATS, THE BEACH

The funeral over, the family
scatters, and sorrow distances itself
with gentle finality. A gather
of friends takes the shore road
north to where steep cliffs, like
sleeping giants, line the coast.
In a diminutive cove, a pocket
of quiet waits, with a dozen bright
kayaks and a rowboat ready
for boarding to paddle out to sea.

It takes time for grief to unfold,
for us to turn the pages of a life,
to allow the story to speak
remembrance and forgiveness
gently into the air, into the heart.

Love and living move away,
diminish. A breaking wave
sweeps and cleanses a beach.

7

AFTER THE STORM

On this day of strenuous wind, the giant gray breakers
rise up, determined to conquer the shore, until, foiled,
they bow their heads, fold their garments of foam, withdraw,
hope to regain enough vigor to try it again, again.
And over again. How oceans love the generous energies
of storms that urge them into frothy delirium,
weaving with strong fingers fluid gowns of lace and
        rainbows,
seeding their endless cresting and obeisance.

How well this sloping shore beneath our feet, this strand
with enough gray pebbles to build an empire,
this plenty of sunlit stones, makes a choir of
glistening sounds as they chant and mutter
under the waves' hands. Overhead, white-headed gulls
claim the fierce air. Below, we listen deep,
praying to be some drop in some wave urged on
in the strong winds of the Weather-maker.

CLUES FOR PERCEPTION

To reverse entropy is to avert chaos, to restore order in a system, to correct or forgive a wrong.

The body, that ancient house for the soul, is a gyration of corpuscles drifting through breakage and blunder. With correction and healing disorder may be reversed.

A shallow hollow in the memory, re-minded and refilled, can resound like a bell ringing.

The cycle: As leaves scatter, fall and rot, soil is enriched and new growth is enabled.

A pink shell of rose petal, that flake of heaven, floats in the warm air, decays, is reconfigured in the ground, thrives into its fresh new bud and bloom.

Summer's dust is only spent pollen.

On the sidewalk, a crumpled candy wrapper gleams its minor version of chaos. When picked up and disposed of, disorder is reversed and chaos declines.

I rejoice when the crumb on the floor falls victim to the broom!

The shattered cup issues a call to glue all the pieces,
restoring possibilities of afternoon tea in the garden.

Random syllables, reordered into words and sentences, may
be rendered intelligible. Every lost word or phrase will finally
recall its meaning.

Shadows will be consumed by the wide mouth of light.

THE QUICKENING: TO BE SUNG IN PROCESSION TO HEAVEN'S GATE

Give praise, now, to our God, the Quickener, the One who stirs us into such new life that we, and all creation, may wake to the sound of a fresh music, and start to sing again the songs of love, and longing, and refreshment. We've waited, silent, for a century, or twenty, so now, for our onward going, may the sun be no longer reluctant, hidden behind clouds, but burnished, un-shadowed, jubilant. It is the Quickener, God's-self, who will awaken us, and all the creation, from lethargy. And it is God-grace at work, reviving us so thoroughly that the stiff, derelict bones within us will stretch and shift and move again freely, with glee, limber and lively, and with more than their usual modicum of seasonal energy. Because God, our Fashioner, will move within us, as all entropy will be halted, all decay reversed.

Come Springtime, that most beneficent of seasons, all, everything, *every thing,* will be thawing, rising, joyful, *laughing,* tuning up for the evermore, and in every green plant, sap will begin again to up-rise, elated. All entropy will be halted, all decay reversed. Nothing remaining will be haphazard, or perverse. On all the twigs of all the trees the buds will begin to burst open in a glory—chestnut, cherry, apple, and apricot—and the maple trees will launch their little helicopter seeds to fly their joy. And in every country's county even the gray, ancient barns will sway in rhythm, settling deeper into their fields, creaking their unison praise under the season's freshening winds. Out on the farm, the old horse will nicker, shaking his white mane at us, we standing by the fence to greet him, one of God's best animals. And on the coast, as the tide in the frost-whiskered creeks creeps in and out again, ducks will nudge each other along on the restless water's gleaming surface, making their quacking duck sounds. At the shore, where ocean, earth, and sky meet in a cosmic triumvirate, the dunes will sweep in and out in a riot of shifting sand, and even the thick brown thatches of kelp will dance with the radiant waves, shrugging their shoulders in maritime rhythms. Whales, those denizens of the waves, grand evidence of the Almighty's sense of humor, will spout and breach for joy, sending up glistens of water into the sun-glancing zephyrs, offering their mighty versions of praise. Let *us* look up now to where eagles ride the wind, viewing landscapes below from the heights of air, yet noticing the small, skittering mouse in the haystack with a precision true of the all-knowing Spirit, Maker of rodents. The tides of entropy have been stayed. Decline is being reversed, and forgotten.

Now, a question: Can a hummingbird sing? Well, on that day she'll be so filled with ecstasy that a creative fervor will nudge her into rhapsodic song! And, below ground, even worms, those earthy annelids, will writhe with subterranean energy, singing their orisons from beneath the sod. Oh, and in Fall, the trees will compose complex arboreal sonnets, lifting their branches, shining, brilliant with leaves of copper and gold. And under the apple trees the ground will boil with a beautiful riot, the squirrels turning tipsy with snacking on the fallen, deliciously fermented fruit. There, and everywhere, *every where,* entropy will have been arrested and decay reversed.

In the cities, the master architects will build cathedrals with spires magnificent in their up-reaching to the Almighty! And painter-pray-ers will write icons, in gold leaf and egg tempera, for penetrating truths whose mythic substance simple words cannot interpret. You and I, and all poets, all wordsmiths and visionaries, will be tasked with body-ing forth the meanings of words like *shine* and *gleam,* *rough* and *glossy, matte* and *refulgent,* words bright with immediacy, glimmer, glance, merriment, invention, fidelity, innocence, resplendence, and benevolence, as together we will create and perform new odes, profound anthems and admirations, and brilliant appreciations of the Lord, our God. The Great Dance has filled heaven's ballroom. Entropy has been reversed. Decline denied entrance, or existence. Death has been utterly extinguished as we enter, and join, the Quickening.

Then we, with the whole passionate earth chorale, with its singers, the oddballs, the trustworthies, the crazed and the rational, will be making music together, performing eternity's spirited oratorios. We'll raise the roof of heaven—all and each of us filled with an intelligent joy, singing songs that we'll know by heart, with an exuberant flow of love foaming over our soul's brims. Entropy will be utterly reversed. Decay will be banished eternally. And together, with our great Conductor, the Holy Spirit, accompanied by lucid voices, and with every enthusiastic instrument ever invented, and then some, we'll make music from an utterly original score, with great jubilation, without ever needing to stop.

ACKNOWLEDGMENTS

Christian Century
"Universe," "Stones," "Leaving,"
"The Quickening"

Ekstasis,
"Leaving," "Weathering," Mary's Sword,"
"Scarlet"

Crux,
"Level," "Mary's Sword"

Whale Road Review,
"The Dance of the Lichens"

"The Dance of the Lichens"
has been nominated for a Pushcart Prize.

About Paraclete Press

Paraclete Press is the publishing arm of the Cape Cod Benedictine community, the Community of Jesus. Presenting a full expression of Christian belief and practice, we reflect the ecumenical charism of the Community and its dedication to sacred music, the fine arts, and the written word.

SCAN
TO
READ
MORE

www.paracletepress.com

IRON
PEN

O that my words were written down!
O that they were inscribed in a book!
O that with an iron pen and with lead
they were engraved on a rock forever!
—JOB 19:23–24

Outcast and utterly alone, Job pours out his anguish to his Maker. From the depths of his pain, he reveals a trust in God's goodness that is stronger than his despair, giving humanity some of the most beautiful and poetic verses of all time. Paraclete's Iron Pen imprint is inspired by this spirit of unvarnished honesty and tenacious hope.

You may also be interested in...

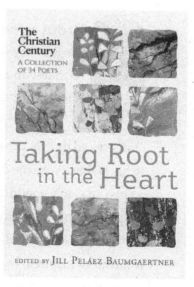
www.paracletepress.com